Picture credits:
l: Left, r: Right, t: Top, b: Bottom, c: Centre

6bl: Elena Elisseeva, 7br: Nicholas Belton.
8t: Andrew F. Kazmierski, 8-9b: Rpernell, 9t: Yonner23, 9m: Bhotting, 10b: PeterG,
11t: Jason Osborne, 11b: Akit, 12-13t: Terry Kettlewell, 12b: Anyka, 13b: Karen Givens,
14t: Stephanie Dankof, 14b: Cathleen Clapper, 15b: Scott Sanders, 16: Alstond | Dreamstime.com,
17: Rebecca Picard, 18-19: Barry Crossley,18b: Westhoff, 20-21: Eifelgrapher, 21b: WilshireImages,
22b: Jack Cronkhite, 23b: Lee torrens, 24t: Patricia Marroquin, 24-25c: Mummu Media, 25t: Kay,
26t: Jeffclow | Dreamstime.com, 27l: Peter Baxter, 27r: Kondrashov MIkhail Evgenevich, 28b: Photosmash,
28-29c: Andrey Armyagov, 30: Jenniferlongley, 31: Kondrashov MIkhail Evgenevich,
32-33: Rodney Mehring, 33b: george green & Barry Crossley, 34t: Paulprescott72,
34b: Lisa Battaglene/ photolibrary, 35: Wendy Kaveney Photography, 38b: Dana Heinemann,
39: Dale A Stork, 42t: MsSponge, 43t: Claudia Steininger, 42-43: marilyn barbone.

Copyright: Really Useful Map Company (HK) Ltd.
Published By: Robert Frederick Ltd.
4 North Parade Bath, England.

First Published: 2006

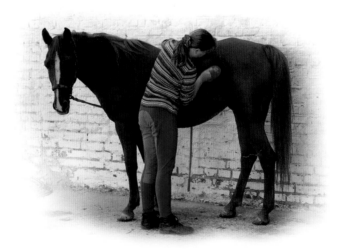

Designed and packaged by
Q2A MEDIA
Printed in China.

Horse and Pony Care

CONTENTS

Understanding Your Horse or Pony

It is not enough to just have a pet horse or pony. You must take proper care to ensure your animal's comfort and health.

First Things First

Your horse or pony neither know you or their new surroundings. So you must first try to form a bond with them. Communicate with them as much as possible and try to understand them. Be affectionate and gentle. Be reassuring so that they can trust you. Do not force them to do things they do not want to. Do not be too tough with them. Remember being a master does not mean that you can bully your pet. Show them around their new home so that they get familiar with their new surrounding. Take extra effort to make them feel protected and cared for.

◀ *Establish a bond of love and trust with your pet*

Make sure you keep the stable clean

To Show you Care

Your responsibility as a master does not end after you bond with your horse or pony. In fact it only begins there. Your horse or pony's health depends on diet, exercise and cleanliness. So you must take good care of what you feed them. You have to find time to take them out for exercise. Keeping them clean is extremely important too. And do not forget to clean their stable. Remember that a hygienic surrounding is the key to good health for everybody.

Top Tips

It is a good idea to let your horse or pony smell your hand so that they recognise your scent. They will become familiar with you this way.

The Stable

The stable is the home for your horse or pony. Remember to design it in a way that is safe and comfortable for them - a place where they would like to stay.

Home Sweet Home

You can make a ready-to-assemble wooden stable or one with bricks. The latter is stronger and safer too. The stable should be airy and roomy. Since horses are bigger they need more space and larger stables than ponies. There should be enough natural light available during the day. It should have an accessible water supply and proper drainage system. Concrete floors are easier to clean so they should be preferred. Straw, paper or Auboise beds can be used as bedding for your horse or pony. The stable should have buckets, hay nets, mangers, as well as tying rings for them. Separate food storage space and tack rooms are important too.

Horses and ponies need clean, safe and comfortable living quarters

Take all necessary precautions to prevent fire in the stable

Safe and Secure

The stable must be safe for your horse or pony. Remember, prevention is better than cure so make sure all electrical fittings are safe with circuit breakers. Hay catches fire easily so store it in a separate space. Keep fire extinguishers in the stable. It is best to have at least two exits out of the stable. To prevent thefts you can put a burglar alarm in the tack room.

Muck breeds disease and must be cleared out daily

Store all the equipment you need to clean the stable in a proper place

Cleanliness is Next to Godliness

The stable should be clean and germ free as dirty stables breed disease. You must muck out every morning: for this you need a wheelbarrow, a shovel, a rake, a fork or shavings scoop, broom, skip or bucket, hose and gloves. Tie the horse or pony outside the stable before you begin cleaning. Clean the bedding as well as the floor and put the muck heap well away from the stable. You must use traps or poison to control rats and mice as they cause damage and spread disease too.

Top Tips

Take every possible care to make sure that the stable for your horse or pony is a safe place for them, do not forget to get your stable insured so that you are reimbursed in case of any accident.

Feeding Well

What you feed your horse or pony determines their wellbeing. They need different types of food to stay healthy and work well. It is important to make sure that they are not eating the same type of food for every meal.

Roughage

Horses and ponies graze on grass in their natural surrounding. However, stabled horses and ponies are fed hay. Hay is the main source of roughage, which is important for their digestive system. It helps to add bulk to the food and is filling. You must feed them good quality hay. Good hay is greenish-brown, sweet smelling and shakes out freely. On average, your horse or pony's diet should contain about 70 per cent roughage.

Horses and ponies enj[oy] feeding on good hay

Concentrates

Apart from hay, your horse or pony needs other nutritious food. These are concentrates - food that give energy for physical labour. Concentrates include oats and barley. Oats can be crushed and fed raw while barley is best fed boiled as it is easily digested in that form. You can even buy concentrate feeds ready-mixed that are suitable for your breed of horse or pony. Concentrates should be about 25-30 per cent of their diet. Avoid feeding concentrates if your horse or pony is at rest, because then the diet can prove too rich for them.

Crushed oats are the best source of concentrates for horses and ponies

Supplements

Stabled horses and ponies need some fresh produce in their diet too. You can either allow them to graze on grass for 10-15 minutes everyday or supplement their diet with fruit and vegetables like apples and carrots. You can feed them yourself to your horse or pony as treats when they behave well. Make sure that you slice them thin, lengthways to avoid any possibility of choking. Fresh food provides your horse or pony with vitamins and minerals that are important for their overall health.

Fruits and vegetables fed in small quantities are good for the overall health of horses and ponies

Top Tips

Horses and ponies need water along with their food. Water not only quenches thirst but helps in digestion too. Make sure to keep adequate fresh water for them in buckets in the stable at all times. Make sure they have access to water if they are grazing outside.

Diet and Routine

In their natural habitat horses and ponies graze over a large area and feed little, but often. When stabled, however, their diet and routine are changed.

How Much and When?

The quantity and quality of feed depend on your horse or pony's size and the kind of work they do. Both under-fed and over-fed horses and ponies will not keep in good health. It is best to know your horse or pony's weight and feed them accordingly. They are usually fed about two percent of their body weight, most of which is roughage. Stabled horses and ponies should be fed twice or thrice in a day and always at the same time.

Things to Remember

- Do not over-feed or under-feed your horse or pony
- Always feed good quality food
- Remember to keep food and water buckets clean
- Never feed your horse or pony just before or after exercise
- Let them graze on fresh grass occasionally
- Remember to add fruit and vegetables in their diet
- Prevent them from drinking too much water immediately after feeding or exercise
- Feed them from your hand to show that you care

Horse and Pony Portions

Since horses are bigger they need more food than ponies. Moreover, ponies have a tendency to gain weight so you must maintain a strict diet for them. Horses generally require more energy-giving concentrates as they work more. Ponies run the risk of foundering much more than horses and should never be fed grain. Bran or husks of wheatgrain are a good alternative for grain and can be fed to both horses and ponies.

Hay can be put in clean buckets or hay nets

Note the difference in size of a horse (right) and pony (left). Being bigger, horses need more feed

Common Questions

Where should I store the food?

You should store your horse or pony's food in a dry place in the stable to keep it fresh. But remember to store it away from the pony!

Pasture Management

Horses and ponies are happiest when they are grazing out on fields. Pastures not only provide the necessary forage that they need but also provide a good exercise area.

Taking Care of Grazing Land

Managing the pasture well is of utmost importance. It requires a lot of time and effort but yields rewards for your horse or pony, as well as you. You need to choose the grass that suits the soil type as well as your horse or pony. They are fond of legumes , so plant some. Use good fertilizers and make sure that you weed the field regularly. Remove droppings to prevent the grass from becoming sour. This also checks the breeding of diseases. Rotating the grazing land replenishes the soil, interrupts the worms' life cycle and reduces infestation.

Fresh, green, juicy grass is every horse and pony's favourite meal!

Fences should be at a height that horses and ponies cannot jump over

Boundaries and Fences

The boundaries of a pasture help to control how much of the paddock your horse and pony have access to. It is best to divide the grazing into at least two sections. Your horse or pony can have access to one paddock while the other can be rested. The fence enclosing your land stops any stray animal from entering or grazing in your field. You must choose the fencing that is safest for your horse or pony. The best option is fence posts and rail fencing, which is usually made of wood. Electric fencing and hedges are the other options. Barbed wire is very dangerous and should never be used.

Shelter and Water

When your horse or pony is turned out to graze, it will need shelter to protect itself from the scorching sun and rain. You can either have a building with a roof in the field or plant lots of trees in the centre of the field to provide natural shelter. Ensuring sufficient water supply is extremely important. Keep a large trough and remember to change the water every day. This is in addition to the water you keep in the stable.

A shelter in the pasture is a must for horses and ponies

! Top Tips

When grass is in abundance, horses and ponies tend to put on weight and run the risk of foundering. Therefore, it is essential to restrict their grazing. It will help if they exercise, but do not make them exercise hard soon after a meal.

Turning Out Horses and Ponies

After you have a good pasture for your horse or pony you need to learn the art of turning them out in the field to graze.

Controlling the Excitement

Most horses and ponies love the prospect of grazing. They get so excited that they tend to run off, dragging you along too! You need to learn to control them to avoid any accident. Use a long lead rope to lead out, as it is easier to control them with that. Avoid turning out over-enthusiastic horses and ponies at the same time every day so that they do not wait in anticipation. You could try giving them a tit-bit so that they wait for it before they run off. If nothing works then simply ride to the paddock, dismount and remove the tack.

Shy Horses and Ponies

Some horses and ponies on the other hand are shy and you may face a difficulty in turning them out. They avoid going out because they are scared. You should try to dispel their fears. Introduce them to the pasture slowly. Keep them where they can see the open field so that they get familiar with it. Put some hay and water in the paddock, take them there, talk to them to reassure them, leave them for a few minutes and fetch them back. They will begin to associate the paddock with food. Then increase the time gradually.

Things to Remember

- *Use enough fly spray on your horse or pony especially during summer, to save them from the nuisance of pests*
- *Cover your horse or pony with a warm blanket when your turn them out in winter*
- *Limit their grazing time to prevent over feeding*
- *Make the pasture a safe place for them with fresh grass free from poisonous weeds, and safe fence and boundary*
- *When you offer a tit-bit be careful how you hold it, as there might be a chance of an enthusiastic horse or pony struggling to get it and hurting you accidentally*
- *Stand beside them when you lead them out and neither pull the rope too hard, nor let it slack - be firm*

!

Top Tips

Remember to wear gloves when you turn out your horse or pony. This will prevent rope burn or cuts in case they pull the rope hard. Remember never to wrap the rope around your hand because, should they run suddenly, you might be dragged along.

Turning out horses and ponies is an art to be learnt!

It is best to have a stable that overlooks a pasture

The Grooming Kit

Did you know that special brushes are available for grooming or cleaning your horse or pony? These brushes are kept together in a plastic box or canvas bag. This is known as the grooming kit.

Grooming Kit List

- *Rubber curry comb: It is used to remove dried mud and loose hair from the pony*
- *Dandy brush: A brush with stiff bristles used to remove dried mud and dirt from the legs*
- *Body brush: It has soft bristles and can be used on the entire body to remove dirt*
- *Metal curry comb: It is used to remove dirt off the body brush during grooming*
- *Mane comb: Plastic or metal combs used to brush the mane and tail*
- *Hoof pick: Usually metal, used for removing dirt and stones from the hooves*
- *Sponges: One for cleaning eyes and nose and the other for the dock area*
- *Sweat scraper: It is used to wipe excess sweat or water off*
- *Linen: A good linen drying-up cloth can be dampened and gently wiped over the body to give it a final polish*

A body brush, gently rubbed, leaves your horse or pony's body shining

A nicely groomed horse looks smart and healthy

Top Tips

Always ensure that you keep all grooming equipment clean. Remove hair from brushes and combs and always clean the sponge after every use. Anything dirty in your grooming kit could lead to a skin disease for your horse or pony.

Keeping Clean

Just as you wash to keep yourself clean, your horse or pony must be kept clean too. Grooming is a very important part of horse and pony care, and must be done very regularly.

Importance of Grooming

Grooming helps to keep your horse or pony neat and tidy. It keeps their coat shiny and makes them look smart. It also helps to keep your horse or pony free from lice. Grooming gently massages your horse or pony, helps to increase blood circulation and builds their muscles. When you groom your horse or pony you can always check carefully for any wounds or sores that it may have and treat them immediately. Grooming also helps to build a good relationship with your horse or pony and shows that you care.

How Often Should I Groom?

You should groom your horse or pony every day, as it gets dirty after exercise. Even if you do not take the horse or pony out for exercise one day, you should not skip grooming. Bathe your horse or pony using good shampoos meant for them. But do that only when it is absolutely essential. Remember to wash them only when the weather is warm. While giving them a bath, do not splash the water all in one go - sprinkle a little water at a time. Use the sweat scraper to wipe off the water, or they might catch a cold. But not giving them a bath does not mean that you skip the grooming. That is absolutely essential. Remember to give your horse or pony a brisk rubdown soon after it has done vigorous exercise, so that the sweat does not stay on the skin.

Dirt and mud must be rubbed off the horse or pony's body with care

Common Questions

Why shouldn't horses and ponies be bathed regularly?

Bathing removes the natural oils from your horse or pony's skin. These oils protect the skin against dirt and even cold. Soaking the coat tends to wash these oils away making your horse or pony vulnerable.

Make sure that the horse or pony does not feel scared when bathed

Things to Remember

- Always tie your pony safely before you begin grooming
- Begin grooming at the shoulder and go up the neck so that your pony knows where you are. Stroke the rubber curry comb firmly, but gently, in the direction of the hair to remove the dirt. Use circular movements to bring out loose hair
- Pick up the Dandy brush and go down the front legs. Be careful! Do not put your face in front of the legs. You may get a knee in your face if your animal picks its leg up suddenly
- Now move towards its barrel, its quarters and its hind legs. Stand close to its quarters while cleaning its hind legs to avoid a kick
- When brushing its face, start from the side so that the animal does not feel scared. Rub off the dirt as gently as possible
- After dried mud and dirt has been removed, use the body brush gently to produce a shine
- Do not forget to brush the mane, preferably with a plastic mane brush. Always comb in the direction of hair
- Comb your animal's tail similarly
- Use a damp sponge to gently clean your animal's eyes, nose and dock area
- For an extra smart look, perhaps before a show, apply some coat gloss and rub off gently

Of Manes and Tails

A thick and shiny mane and tail add to your horse or pony's beauty. However, if they are unkempt, they can make your horse or pony look very untidy.

Combing

Always use plastic and not metal combs for your horse or pony. Brush down in sections to remove the tangles. Do not pull too hard. While combing the tail, stand to one side and pull the tail gently towards you to avoid an accidental kick from your horse or pony. You can use a grooming spray that helps to detangle the hair easily.

Washing

Manes and tails tend to get dirty and greasy. It becomes essential to wash them at such times. Remember to wash them only when the weather is warm. Dampen the mane and tail in lukewarm water and then wash with a good quality shampoo. Make sure that the shampoo does not get into your horse or pony's eyes, ears or nose. Rinse off the shampoo and dry with a towel. You can swing the tail to remove excess water. Do it gently. Do not forget to brush the mane and the tail after a wash.

Many horse and pony owners spend a lot of time in beautifying their horse or pony's mane and tail

'Pulling' Manes and Tails

Most horses and ponies have thick manes and tails that can get unmanageable. It is for this reason that manes and tails need to be 'pulled' or thinned. It is best to pull the mane and tail after exercise as the pores are open at this time and excess hair comes out easily. Remove tangles from the hair then wind a few hairs at a time around the comb and pull sharply downwards. Work on it until it looks neat. Remember to pull only a small area every day and work over a week or two for a tidy look.

The illustration shows how manes and tails are to be pulled

Common Questions

Can't I just cut my pony's mane and tail?

Never use scissors or clippers to cut your horse or pony's mane and tail. Cutting or trimming can ruin their appearance and make them appear even thicker.

Horse and pony manes can be thinned for their comfort especially during summers

Hoof Care

Your horse or pony's feet need a lot of special care as they rely on their feet to do all the work.

My Shoes are the Best!

Horses and ponies began wearing shoes hundreds of years back when man domesticated them. Shoes protect their hooves when they travel long distances at great speed and carry loads. Nowadays, several types of shoes are available for your horse or pony. Shoes, such as egg-bar or straight-bar, are specially designed to correct any particular foot problem that your horse or pony may have. Fuller shoes are most commonly used for horses and ponies. Extra-grip shoes can be used on horses and ponies that work hard especially on hilly roads or compete on slippery grass.

Shoeing

Your horse and pony must wear properly fitted shoes. For this they need to be shod every six to eight weeks. Regular shoeing prevents disease and lameness among horses and ponies. You must contact a farrier to shoe your horse and pony. He will trim the hooves and shape the shoes to ensure that the shoes are comfortable for them. He will also be able to offer corrective shoeing if that is necessary, so that over the time your horse and pony's feet become healthier. If a shoe comes off for some reason, you must get it replaced immediately.

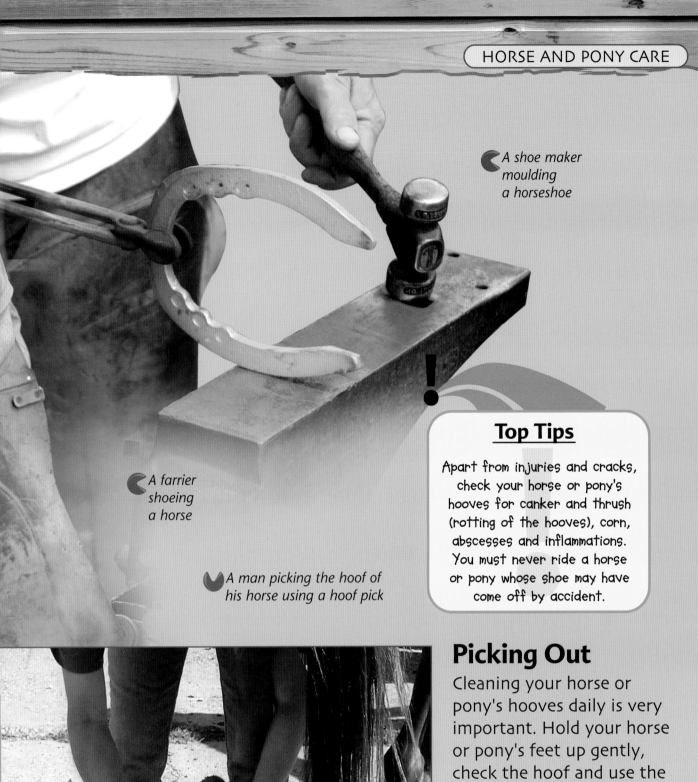

A shoe maker moulding a horseshoe

A farrier shoeing a horse

A man picking the hoof of his horse using a hoof pick

Top Tips

Apart from injuries and cracks, check your horse or pony's hooves for canker and thrush (rotting of the hooves), corn, abscesses and inflammations. You must never ride a horse or pony whose shoe may have come off by accident.

Picking Out

Cleaning your horse or pony's hooves daily is very important. Hold your horse or pony's feet up gently, check the hoof and use the hoof pick to pick out dirt, pebbles or anything else stuck in the sole of the foot. Remember to check for any injury, infection or cracks and consult your farrier in case of any problem. Repeat the process for all four feet.

Keeping Fit

Exercise keeps your horse
or pony healthy and fit.
Horses and ponies are built
for life on the move so you must exercise
them every day, except when they are ill.

Since you stand in the middle and instruct your horse or pony, lunging teaches it to pay attention to you

Beginning with the Basics

Tack up your horse or pony before exercise. Do not forget to wear proper gear yourself. Now sit up straight on the saddle, keeping your knees bent and heels down. Relax your arms when you hold the reins. It is a good idea to stretch yourself a bit before you mount your horse or pony. Now begin the exercise of riding by walking them. Instead of a full riding exercise every day, you can occasionally lunge them in a circle around you, remembering to change the direction regularly. This allows the horse or pony to exercise without having to carry extra weight.

On the move

Always begin your horse or pony's exercises with warm-up walks and increase the workload gradually. Encourage them to keep steady as they walk by giving them proper riding aids or signals. A walk should ideally last about 20 minutes after which you can trot them. Build up the pace gradually. Short periods of galloping help to build their stamina. But do not overburden them. Allow them to cool off after fast exercise by walking them slowly. A combination of walk, trot and gallop is the best exercise for your horse or pony, but keep the gallop to a minimum.

Good Riding

Try to supply as many movements to your horse or pony as possible. Make it move in circles and serpentine ways. Walking on roads makes their tendons and muscles stronger, but you must ensure that your horse or pony is comfortable moving on roads and you are well versed in road safety procedures. Do not exercise your horse or pony immediately after a feed or shot. Their hooves must be picked before and after every ride. Just as you enjoy Sundays, give your horse and pony a rest day too.

Take all road safety precautions when you ride on the road

Good riding is that which is comfortable for both you and your horse or pony

Common Questions

What is the Pony Express?

The Pony Express was a mail system that began in April 1960 in old western America where the riders rode without rest to deliver mail. It was the fastest mail system of that time till telegraph was introduced a year later in November. Predictably, the horses that were made to work so hard fell ill and lived only a quarter as long as normal horses.

Summer Care

Summer heat can be hard on your horse or pony. Some basic attention can ensure their comfort and health in the warm weather.

Along the neck

Along the withers

Clipping

Horses and ponies tend to grow more hair in winter. The thick coat can be troublesome in the warm weather so you need to clip or shear them. Clipping will ensure that they cool down quickly after exercise and riding. Depending on your horse or pony's workload, you can choose the type of clip you want. It is advisable to take professional help for clipping your horse and pony.

What a Nuisance!

Flies and mosquitoes are common in summer. They are not just a bother but also breed diseases, so you need to protect your horse against them. The use of fly blankets and sprays helps to reduce these pests. Be careful not to spray in your horse or pony's eyes, nose or mouth. Keep muck heaps well away from the stable to reduce flies.

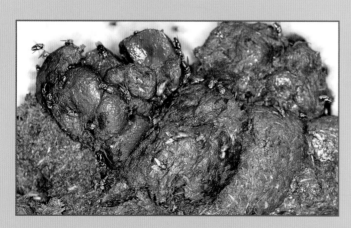

Flies breeding on manure can carry many diseases

The image shows a clipped horse. This is called the hunter clip where hair is left intact around the saddle area and the legs

Crease down the loin

Tailhead

?

Common Questions

What are the various clips for horses and ponies?

The blanket clip, hunter clip, full clip, trace clip and belly and gullet clip are the various options in clipping.

Ribs

Behind the shoulder

A clipper used to shave the horse or pony

Things to Remember

- Keep enough fresh water for your horse or pony to drink
- You may reduce its diet a little and feed it at cooler hours of the day
- Use sun block, especially for grey horses and ponies, to prevent sunburn
- Give them some salt as there is a chance of dehydration
- If fresh grass is not available, feed them alfalfa, as they need green food in summers
- Hang a fan in the stable in a safe position to cool it off
- Sponge the horse or pony during excessive heat

Keeping Warm

Domestic horses and ponies are dependent on us for keeping them warm and protecting them against freezing winters. You have to be careful to do this to avoid any serious illness.

A warm rug is a must during winters as it keeps the horse or pony cozy

I am Cozy

Several types of rugs are available for your horse or pony's comfort. Choose rugs made from natural fibres like wool and jute. Synthetic rugs lined with cotton are easier to clean, so some people prefer them. Night rugs should be thick and warm. Rugs you use during the day should be thinner. Special exercise rugs are used when you take your horse or pony for exercise or a ride in winters. These are placed under the saddle. Rugs usually have cross-over straps. Make sure that you do not tie them too tight, and that the horse or pony is able to breathe easily.

Cleaning the Rugs

Just as you clean your jackets and quilts, your horse or pony's rugs need to be cleaned too. For this you must ensure that you have at least one spare night and day rug that you can use while you wash the first one. Rugs are best cleaned in a washing machine. Remember to follow the manufacturer's washing instructions when you clean the rugs. After the grease and dirt has been removed from the rugs, rinse them and hang them out to dry.

Winter Care

Wild horses and ponies develop natural protection against winter. However, stabled horses and ponies need special attention. Apart from using rugs to keep them warm, their hooves need to be checked thoroughly in winters. If you are riding out, avoid icy and frozen ground and try to limit yourself to walking the horse or pony. Carry a hoof pick and stop periodically to pick out the ice from its soles. Brush your horse and pony often as it provides insulation. Feed them more hay for extra calories that will keep them warm. Remember to keep the drinking water warm. Or they may not want to drink it even when they should.

Top Tips

Regular de-worming is essential in winter as equine parasites are difficult to kill in cold weather. Consult your veterinarian for de-worming doses.

Horses and ponies must be ridden at a slow speed on snow

Tack Care

You need some basic equipment and accessories when you ride your horse or pony. This is known as tack. Tack helps you sit comfortably and control your horse or pony well.

Bridle

Tack it Up

The tack consists of the bridle and the saddle.
You will sit on the saddle when you ride, so it needs to be comfortable. You should also keep in mind your horse or pony's comfort when you choose a saddle. The saddle should not be hard on their back. The bridle is a set of leather straps that includes a headstall, bit and rein, all of which are fitted about your horse or pony's head.

Cleaning the Bridle

Tack should be cleaned and checked for wear and tear. Cleaning the tack regularly keeps it in good condition and makes it long lasting. Remove the bridle from the horse or pony's head. Use a damp sponge to remove the dirt and grease from the leather straps. Check carefully for any cracks on the leather. Do not forget to check the seams to check if the stitching is sound. If any part needs mending do it immediately. Wash the bit separately in soapy water and dry it with a clean cloth. Now use saddle soap and a cloth to polish all the leather straps. Likewise, use metal polish on metallic parts but avoid parts that come in contact with the horse or pony's mouth.

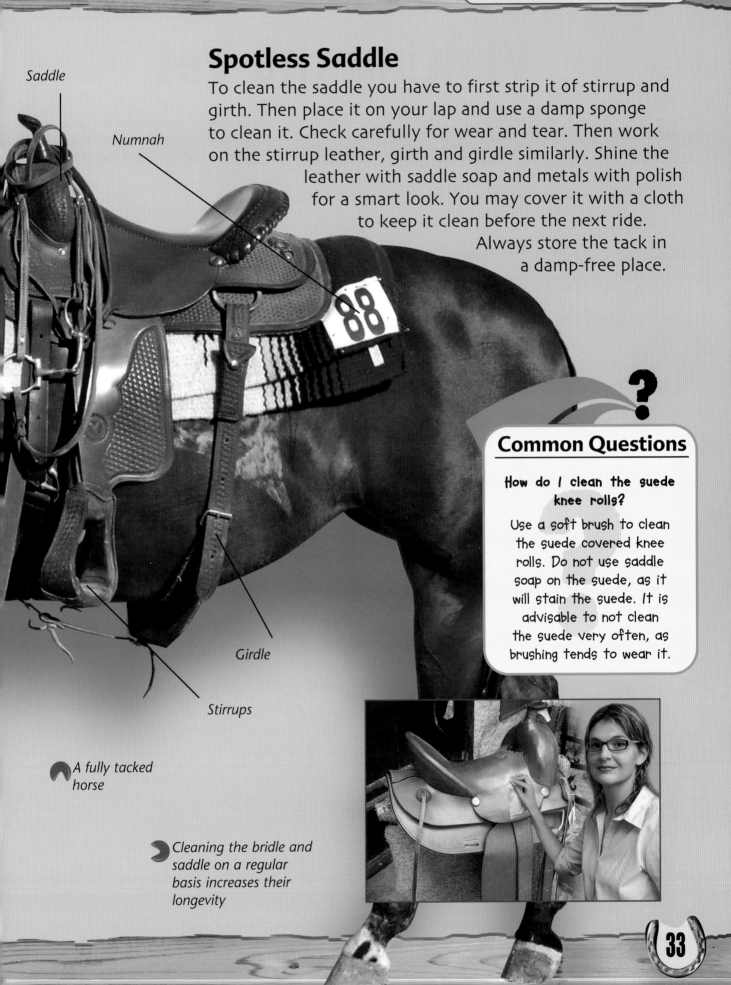

Spotless Saddle

To clean the saddle you have to first strip it of stirrup and girth. Then place it on your lap and use a damp sponge to clean it. Check carefully for wear and tear. Then work on the stirrup leather, girth and girdle similarly. Shine the leather with saddle soap and metals with polish for a smart look. You may cover it with a cloth to keep it clean before the next ride. Always store the tack in a damp-free place.

Saddle

Numnah

Girdle

Stirrups

A fully tacked horse

Cleaning the bridle and saddle on a regular basis increases their longevity

Common Questions

How do I clean the suede knee rolls?

Use a soft brush to clean the suede covered knee rolls. Do not use saddle soap on the suede, as it will stain the suede. It is advisable to not clean the suede very often, as brushing tends to wear it.

Visiting the Vet

Just as you have a doctor who checks you regularly, your horse or pony needs veterinary attention too; you must fix a vet for their treatment and care. They should check the health of your horse or pony regularly and give it all the shots needed.

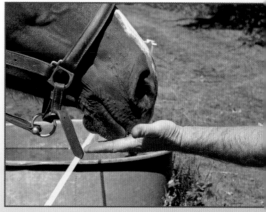
A man feeding de-wormer to a horse

Annual Shots

A vet examining a horse with a stethoscope

It is said that prevention is better than cure. Your horse or po does not only need a vet when they are sick or have an injury Since they are at risk to diseases all the time, they need some preventative medicines to keep good health. They need to be guarded against tetanus and equine influenza and require annual vaccinations for the prevention of these. Other annu vaccinations include anti- EEE WEE VEE and anti-rabies shots. The vet maintains a medical chart for your horse pony so you know when a shot is due.

Regular Doses

Apart from annual shots a regular de-worming programme is a must as your horse or pony can pick up worms while grazing. If not treated these worms can be extremely harmful for them. De-worming is done every six weeks, but at certain times of the year it is done more often. Wormers usually come in powders that can be mixed into feed. You must ensure that your horse or pony eats them. Most horses and ponies do not make a fuss about their medicine. But if they do, try giving them the medicine with a cube of sugar.

Million-Dollar Smile

Dental care is as important for your horse or pony as other treatments. Infections in gums is not only painful but breeds several diseases too. You must check their teeth during grooming and call the vet incase of any dental problem. The teeth of your horse or pony need to be floated regularly: floating refers to the rasping and smoothing of teeth that develop sharp edges due to constant chewing. With the advancement in instruments, equine dentistry has improved greatly, to the benefit of your horse or pony.

A horse or pony's dental care is important for its overall health

Top Tips

Horses and ponies with dental problems will show some signs. Apart of external inflammation of gums, they will eat less and there will be more undigested food material in their dung. They might emit a foul odour from their mouth. There might even be swelling of the face. They will tend to toss their heads and chew the bit. It is important to identify dental problems early and treat them properly.

Sick Horses and Ponies

Healthy horses and ponies have lustrous coats. They are bright and alert and respond to every sound and move.

Are you Ill?

As you form a bond with your horse or pony, you will know instinctively when they are ill. Your horse or pony will also send out signals to convey that they are ill - you simply have to learn to recognise them.

Master Doctor

Recognising that your horse or pony is ill is part of your responsibility as their master. You cannot call a vet all the time and so must learn to check their basic health yourself. You can watch out for external injuries when you groom your horse or pony. Apart from this you should learn to recognise their breathing pattern and pulse beat. You can place your palms on their ribcage to feel the breathing. A good place to check the pulse is at the throat. If the breathing and pulse are faster or slower than normal then your horse or pony might be sick. You must learn to use a veterinary thermometer to check their temperature.

A veterinary thermometer

Sickness Signs

- Excessive sweating
- Cloudy, red or rolling eyes
- Discharge from the nose
- Ears lying flat
- Dull coat
- Heavy breathing
- Excessive rolling
- Pecking at the stomach
- Disinterested and irritable
- Inability to stand on all four legs or move
- Loose or no motions

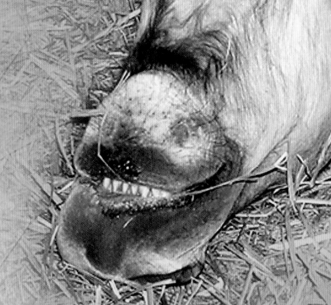

A sick horse or pony must be cared for and given proper medical attention

Common Diseases

Most horses and ponies suffer from some common health problems. Colic or abdominal pain is a frequent complaint. This can happen due to problems in diet or worms. Flu is as much a bother for them as it is for you and me and must be treated well. Laminitis or swelling and inflammation of the feet, leading to lameness, is more common in ponies. The utmost care, as well as medication, is needed to treat it. Various skin problems too may bother horses and ponies and have to be treated accordingly.

?

Common Questions

What are the normal breathing and pulse rates of horses and ponies?

At rest a horse or pony's breathing rate is between 8–16 breaths per minute, while normal pulse rate is between 36–40 beats per minute.

First Aid

You must have a first aid kit in your stable. You should also learn the basics of giving first aid before the vet arrives in cases of emergency and injury.

In Case of a Fall

A first aid box or kit with all the essential products is a must for every stable

One thing you must always remember is to not panic, even in the case of the worst emergency. It is important that you stay calm; only then will your horse or pony be calm. Do not move the horse or pony unless it is absolutely essential to do so. Remember, if they have got a fracture then moving around is not only painful but dangerous too. Call the vet. Make sure that you gather your horse or pony's vital signs before the vet arrives so as to give him the information. Reassure your horse or pony until the vet comes.

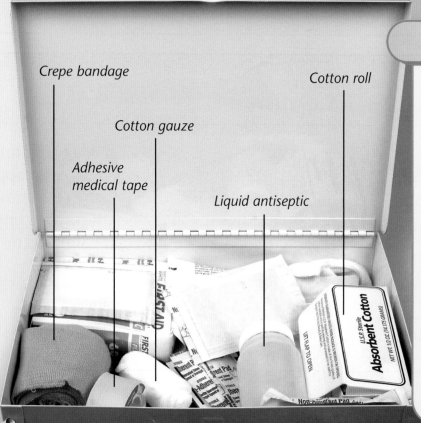

Crepe bandage

Cotton roll

Cotton gauze

Adhesive medical tape

Liquid antiseptic

First Aid Kit

- Large roll of cotton
- Rolls of cotton gauze
- Rolls of crepe bandage
- Adhesive medical tape
- Salt
- Wound powder
- Liquid antiseptic
- Antiseptic cream
- Veterinary thermometer
- Scissors
- Tweezers
- Clean bowl
- Torch
- A syringe of Tetanus Antitoxin and a Tetanus booster in the refrigerator

Flesh Wounds

First of all, locate the wound and the nature of the injury. When you have identified it, act quickly. First clean the wound with clean water to remove dirt and debris. Then use saline water or antiseptic liquid to cleanse it thoroughly and prevent infection. Repeat till you are sure that the wound is clean. Use cotton to apply antiseptic cream in the area. If the wound is not too deep keep it open, otherwise dress it with gauze. If the wound is deep pad it with a sterile padding and if bleeding continues call the vet.

!

Top Tips

The basic first aid principles are to catch and calm the horse or pony, assess the extent of the injury, give proper first aid, gather their vital signs and then seek veterinary advice. Remember to replace tetanus syringes when the expiry date is over. Only attempt to give your horse or pony a shot if you are trained to do so.

All injuries to your horse or pony must be treated without any delay

Nursing Sick Horses and Ponies

Just as you need your parents to nurse and take care of you when you are sick, your horse or pony too needs proper care and time when they are ill or injured. First of all you need to assess your horse or pony's ailment because its care will depend on it. Then proceed with its nursing accordingly.

- If you have other animals in the stable, it is best to separate the sick horse or pony, especially if it has influenza, to prevent contagion

- Consult your vet about the kind of feed you should provide the sick horse or pony

- Sometimes you may have to mix medicines with feed. You must ensure that your horse or pony intakes it

- Keeping sick horses and ponies clean is very important, so you must groom them even when they are sick

- Keep the stable clean and hygienic. Remove muck from the bedding to prevent the breeding of disease

- The sick horse or pony's exercise depends on the kind of disease and injury. If the complaint is colic, they are made to run as it cures them. Horses and ponies suffering from influenza can also be exercised provided they are not running very high temperatures. However, exercise is absolutely forbidden for those who have fractured their bones, unless the vet advises it

- In the case of a flesh wound, ask the vet how often you need to dress it and work on their advice

- You must keep checking them to see how well they are healing

- Your attention and time are as important as medicines, so remember to be there with your sick horse or pony to calm and reassure them and to provide a healing touch

A sick horse looks weak, dull and inattentive

?

Common Questions

Do I need to take some precautions for myself during nursing my sick horse or pony?

You should ensure that you do not carry germs to your sick horse or pony, nor catch any infection from them yourself. Nurse and feed them with clean hands. For your safety cover your mouth while cleaning muck. Remember to wash your hands with antiseptic solution after dressing your horse or pony.

Loving Your Horse or Pony

You can best form a bond with your horse or pony by handling it frequently. Remember they are your responsibility and you need to love and take care of them.

I'm Here For You

Your horse or pony needs your time and attention. Be a parent to them. Horses and ponies respond well to words — so talk to them and also remember to listen to what they say. Do not be too pushy. Be gentle, compassionate but firm. Let it smell your hand often so that it recognises your scent. You must show your affection physically by stroking it gently and feeding it from your own hands.

Your horse or pony can be your best friend — you must love and care for it well!

Don't be Scared

When your horse or pony is new to the surroundings, you must make them feel at home. Take time out to show them around so that they get familiar with their new home. You must be patient with them. Do not be harsh or forceful. Reassure them constantly to dispel their fears. Never approach them from behind or suddenly as this scares them. Make your presence felt by talking gently as you approach them from the side. Just as you do not like to be yelled at, horses and ponies do not like to be shouted at either.

Top Tips

You must maintain a good balance of compassion and firmness with horses and ponies. Never beat them. You can show a whip to direct them but never hit them. A horse or pony treated gently will respond to your commands far better than others.

See how a little child is leading her pony

Be there with your horse or pony so that they trust you

Trust me Dear

You must handle your horse or pony in a way that helps them trust you. Grooming them daily and taking care of them will convince your horse or pony of your love for them and they will trust you. You are their new master, be a leader. You need to be firm but never aggressive. If they get stubborn, reassure them first. If they continue to misbehave then be stern and direct them well. They will learn whatever you teach them.

Glossary

Abscess: A swelling with pus
Adequate: Enough
Accessible: Readily available
Assess: To evaluate
Circuit breaker: An automatic safety device for stopping the flow of current in an electric circuit
Clipping: Trimming the body hair of horses and ponies
Constitution: Physical build
Contagion: Communication of disease from one person to another
Dismount: To get off a horse or pony
Dispel: Make (a doubt or feeling) disappear
Equine: Relating to the horse family
Fertilizer: A chemical added to soil to increase its fertility

Founder: A disease causing lameness
Grooming: Cleaning

Hay manger: Trough for feeding hay to horses and ponies
Infestation: Germs and disease causing organisms on the body or in a place

Legumes: Plants belonging to the pea family
Longevity: Long life
Lunging: The process where you stand while you have your horse lope or trot, or even walk, around you in a circle
Muck out: Clearing out the dung from the stable
Pasture: Land covered mainly with grass suitable for grazing
Prospect: Possibility of any future event
Reimbursed: To be paid money back
Replenish: To restore back to original state
Serpentine: Winding and twisting

Index